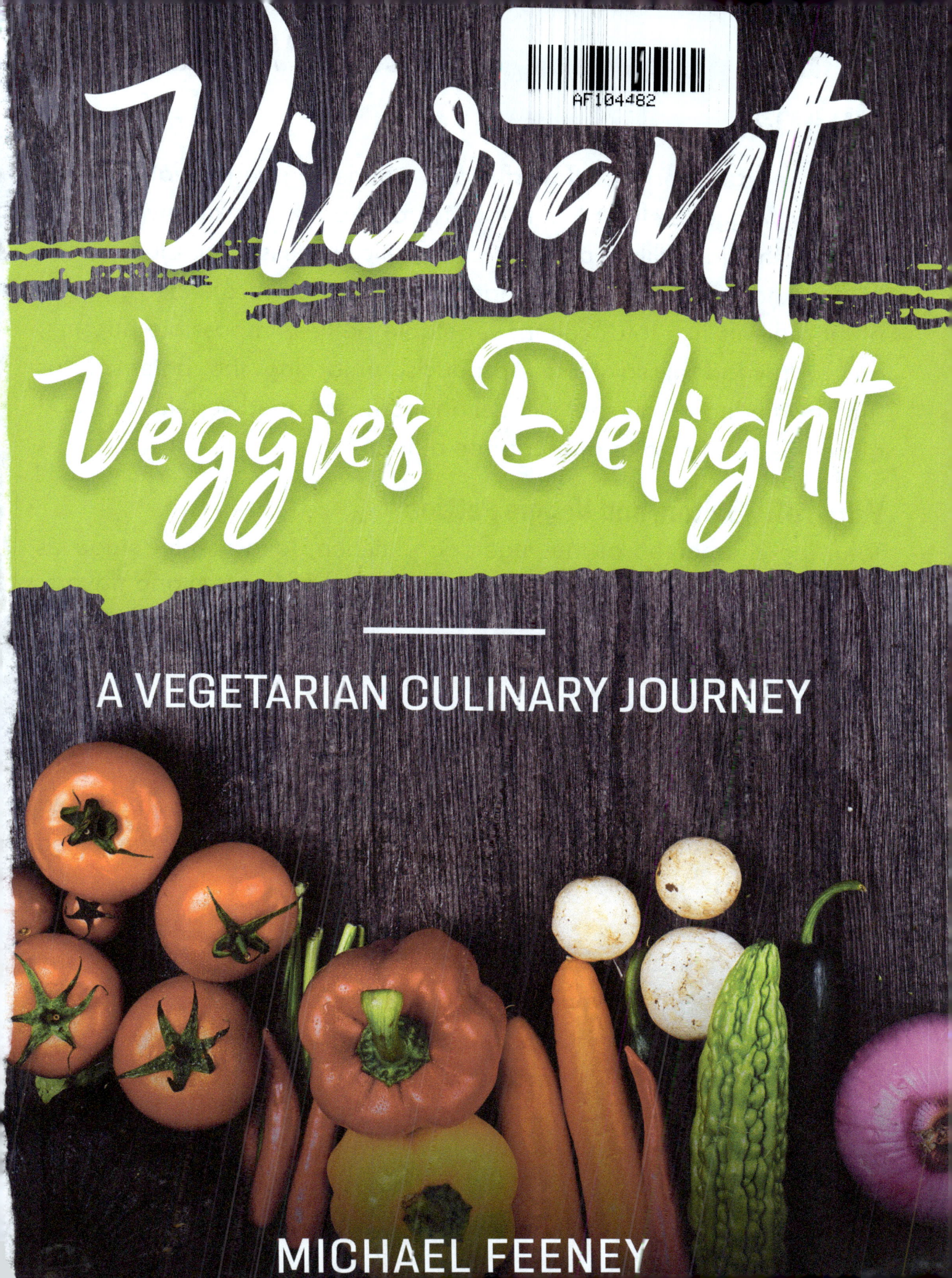

"Vibrant Veggie Delights: A Vegetarian Culinary Journey"

Welcome to a world of flavorful and nourishing vegetarian cuisine! "Vibrant Veggie Delights" is not just a cookbook; it's an invitation to explore the incredible diversity and deliciousness that plant-based cooking has to offer. In this culinary journey, we celebrate the versatility of ingredients like tofu, Seitan, vegetable patties, impossible burgers, and a myriad of soy-based products, unlocking the potential for mouthwatering meals that will delight both seasoned vegetarians and those new to the world of meat-free dining.

Why Tofu, Seitan, and Veggie Patties?

Tofu, the chameleon of the vegetarian kitchen, takes center stage as we unveil its ability to transform into a myriad of textures and flavors. Whether silky smooth in a dessert or crisply grilled in a savory dish, tofu is a protein-packed canvas ready to absorb the essence of your favorite seasonings.

Seitan, the hearty wheat protein, adds a satisfying chewiness to your meals. Discover its robust character as we guide you through crafting delectable Seitan-based dishes that will leave even the most dedicated carnivores craving more.

Vegetable patties, a celebration of the bountiful harvest, showcase the incredible variety of flavors and colors Mother Nature provides. From quinoa and black bean burgers to zucchini and chickpea patties, our recipes will redefine your understanding of what a satisfying veggie burger can be.

Beyond the Burger: The Impossible and Soy Revolution

Embark on a culinary adventure as we delve into the world of plant-based innovation with the Impossible Burger and an array of soy-based products. These creations offer a taste of the future, where sustainability meets mouthwatering flavor. From stir-fries infused with soy goodness to the revolutionary Impossible Burger , my recipes will make you rethink what's possible in the realm of vegetarian cooking.

Embrace the Green Revolution

"Vibrant Veggie Delights" isn't just about recipes; it's about embracing a lifestyle that is both compassionate and scrumptious. Join us in creating meals that not only nourish your body but also contribute to a greener, more sustainable planet. Whether you're a committed vegetarian or just looking to incorporate more plant-based meals into your diet, this cookbook is your guide to a world of culinary possibilities.

Get ready to embark on a gastronomic journey where vegetables take the spotlight, and every dish is a celebration of flavor, innovation, and the joy of conscious eating. Let the cooking begin!

Contents

05 SEITAN BASIC PREPARATION

08 BROTHS

12 TOFU PREPARATION

19 IMPOSSIBLE BURGERS

25 JACKFRUIT IMPOSSIBLE BURGER.

28 TEMPEH

31 MAJOR SOY PRODUCTS AVAILABLE

33 VEGETARIAN RECIPES

64 BREADS

69 SUMMARY

71 ABOUT THE AUTHOR

Seitan BASIC PREPARATION

The primary ingredient for your favorite new meat substitute is Whole Wheat Gluten. Preferably you will need to find a good organically grown whole wheat flour. This will be either Spring or Winter Wheat with Spring Wheat having a softer consistency. The fresher your flour the more cooperative the gluten will be in the separation process.

First the flour is mixed into a FIRM dough preferably in a mixer with warm water. Using cold water causes the gluten to constrict making it take longer to separate the grain and starch. The amount of gluten can vary. So as far as measurement goes you can go by using enough water to create a firm dough. When this is completed place the dough in a container large enough to hold at least two times as much water to cover the dough ball. Let this sit for at least an hour to give the dough ball time to bond and expand slightly.

The second step is to separate the gluten from the starch and grain. This is accomplished by kneading the dough in the water. The water will turn white from the starch leaving the dough ball. When the water has thickened up a bit (after about five minutes of kneading) pour out the water while leaving the dough ball behind. If the gluten breaks up on you let it settle and continue to knead. Another trick is a bit of cheese cloth in a colander but continuing to knead in the water will cause the ball to firm up. Replace fresh water and repeat the process until all starch is removed. There will be a bit of grain in the ball but the fiber can't hurt. The more you knead the more grain will fall from the dough ball giving more of a silky texture.

Fresh flour will be easier to work with but if the grain content is high the dough tends to break up in the water due to the grain interfering with the gluten bonding. The best way to handle this problem is to knead the dough in a colander suspended in water allowing the grain to sink.

Another simple way is a mixer with a dough hook set on a low speed in the sink with water running into the bowl. Yes, whole wheat gluten is generally available for purchase. Gluten is the protein found in wheat and other grains like barley and rye. Whole wheat gluten specifically comes from whole wheat flour, which includes the grain, germ, and endosperm of the wheat kernel.

You can typically find whole wheat gluten in the baking or health food sections of grocery stores. It may be sold as vital wheat gluten or simply as wheat gluten. Additionally, you can find it in some specialty or health food stores. If you're having trouble finding it locally, you may also consider checking online retailers or specialty food websites.

VIBRANT VEGGIE DELIGHTS: A VEGETARIAN CULINARY JOURNEY

Seitan, a popular meat substitute made from gluten, is commonly associated with East Asian cuisines, particularly in China and Japan. In these cultures, Seitan has been used for centuries as a protein source in vegetarian and vegan diets. In Chinese cuisine, it is often referred to as "mianjin," while in Japanese cuisine, it is known as "fu" or "hikiwari."

Additionally, Seitan has gained popularity in Western countries, where vegetarian and vegan diets are more prevalent. It is commonly used in vegetarian and vegan dishes as a meat alternative due to its meaty texture and ability to absorb flavors. In Western cultures, Seitan is often found in vegetarian and vegan restaurants, as well as in the homes of individuals following plant-based diets.

While Seitan may not be as widespread in certain cultures, its popularity has been growing globally as more people explore vegetarian and vegan lifestyles or seek alternatives to meat for various reasons.

My favorite way to cook Seitan is to definitely boil it first then cook another way after.

BROTHS

The broths for boiling Seitan can be just about any broth but I would recommend a clear one (not pre-thickened). A loose broth finds its way into the small cavities that occur during the boiling process infusing it with flavor. These cavities later shrink with cooling. When boiling Seitan make sure you have a rolling boil and add the pieces separately to prevent sticking. A stir or two will also help, just like pasta.

Basic Kombu Broth Traditional

- 5 cups water
- ¾ cups Shoyu or Tamari
- 2 oz fresh Ginger Root
- 2 oz Dried Kombu

Finely chop the ginger and add to the wet ingredients along with the Kombu. Do not pre soak the Kombu to rehydrate before adding to the broth as salt and flavor will be dissolved. Vegetable broth is a versatile and flavorful base for many dishes. Some popular vegetable broth options include:

- **Homemade Vegetable Broth:** Making your own vegetable broth allows you to control the ingredients and flavors. You can use a variety of vegetables such as onions, carrots, celery, garlic, and herbs like thyme and parsley.

- **Store-Bought Options:** If you prefer convenience, there are many good-quality store-bought vegetable broths available. Look for low-sodium or no-added MSG options for a healthier choice.

- **Vegetable Bouillon Cubes or Powder:** These are concentrated forms of vegetable broth that can be convenient for quick use. Be sure to check the ingredients for any additives or preservatives.

- **Mushroom Broth:** If you enjoy a deeper, umami flavor, consider using mushroom broth as a base. It adds a rich and savory taste to dishes

Seitan Is A Versatile Meat Substitute.
Here Are Ten Recipes For Preparing Seitan:

Basic Seitan

- Mix 1 cup vital wheat gluten, 1/4 cup nutritional yeast, and spices (such as garlic powder, onion powder, and paprika) in a bowl.
- Add 3/4 cup water and knead into a dough.
- Simmer the dough in Kombu broth for 30 minutes. After separating from the starch.

Seitan Stir Fry

- Cut Seitan into strips.
- Sauté with vegetables (bell peppers, broccoli, carrots) in a pan.
- Add soy sauce, ginger, and garlic for flavor to taste.

BBQ Seitan Ribs

- Cut Seitan into rib-shaped pieces.
- Brush with BBQ sauce and bake until caramelized.

Seitan Curry

- Cut Seitan into chunks and add to your favorite curry.
- Simmer until the Seitan absorbs the flavors.

Buffalo Seitan Bites

- Cut Seitan into bite-sized pieces.
- Toss in buffalo sauce and bake until crispy.

VIBRANT VEGGIE DELIGHTS: A VEGETARIAN CULINARY JOURNEY

Seitan Tacos

- Crumble Seitan and sauté with taco seasoning.
- Fill taco shells with Seitan, lettuce, salsa, and guacamole.

Lemon Herb Seitan Cutlets

- Flatten Seitan into cutlets.
- Marinate in lemon juice, olive oil, and herbs.
- Grill or pan-fry until golden.

Teriyaki Seitan Skewers

- Cut Seitan into cubes.
- Thread onto skewers and brush with teriyaki sauce.
- Grill or bake until browned.

Seitan and Vegetable Kebabs

- Alternate Seitan chunks with vegetables on skewers.
- Grill or roast until the veggies are tender.

Mushroom and Onion Seitan Steaks

- Mix finely chopped mushrooms, onions, and garlic with Seitan.
- Form into steak shapes and grill or pan-fry.

Feel free to customize these recipes to your taste preferences, and enjoy exploring.

TOFU PREPARATION

Ah, the magical journey of tofu creation – where soybeans embark on a transformation from edamame to the Big Dog of the vegetarian protein world.

Once upon a soybean field, the soybeans gathered for a secret midnight meeting and decided they were destined for greatness. With a wink and a nod, they huddled together and whispered, "Let's become tofu!"

Enter the tofu alchemist, armed with a cauldron and a wand (okay, maybe just a blender). The soybeans, now dressed in tiny superhero capes, dive into a hot tub of water. This is their spa day.

The alchemist then performs the ancient art of soybean yoga, blending and stretching the beans into a smooth, creamy concoction. This soy milk is the elixir of tofu life. The alchemist adds a touch of magic coagulant (usually a mineral called gypsum or a sea salt derivative) to make the soy milk curdle and transform into curds. It's a dairy-free dairy farm in that cauldron.

Now, the tofu curds need to be pressed.

Use any fine mesh colander or one lined with cheesecloth to drain off excess liquid.

And voila! Tofu is born – a blank canvas for culinary creativity.

Now, let's dive into three epic tofu recipes that will have you doing the tofu twist in the kitchen:

Tofu Warrior Stir Fry

- Marinate tofu cubes in soy sauce, ginger, and garlic – let them soak up the flavors.
- Stir-fry with a colorful army of veggies – broccoli, bell peppers, and carrots are your loyal sidekicks.
- Add a splash of teriyaki sauce and a sprinkle of sesame seeds for that extra kick.

Tofu Sympathy Salad

- Crumble tofu into a bowl like you're creating a tofu symphony – let those curds sing!
- Toss with mixed greens, cherry tomatoes, and avocado for a harmonious blend of flavors.
- Drizzle with a balsamic vinaigrette – a dressing so good it could make a celery stick taste like dessert.

- Slice tofu into stealthy strips and marinate in a spicy soy-ginger sauce
- Stir-fry with udon noodles, snap peas, and a sprinkle of crushed red pepper—the heat is your ninja battle cry.
- Finish with a squeeze of lime and a sprinkle of green onions

Meat Substitues

There are numerous meat substitutes available, catering to different taste preferences and nutritional requirements. Here's a list of the most common meat substitutes:

- **Tofu:** Made from soybeans, tofu is a versatile and protein-rich meat substitute. It takes on the flavor of the ingredients it's cooked with
- **Tempeh:** Another soy-based product, tempeh is made by fermenting cooked soybeans. It has a firmer texture and nuttier flavor than tofu.
- **Seitan:** Also known as wheat gluten, Seitan is a protein-rich meat substitute made from gluten, the protein in wheat. It has a chewy texture and can be seasoned to mimic the taste of meat.
- **Legumes:** Beans, lentils, and chickpeas are excellent sources of protein and can be used in various dishes as meat substitutes.
- **Mushrooms:** Portobello mushrooms, in particular, have a hearty texture and can be grilled or roasted to resemble meat. Mushrooms are also often used in plant-based burgers.
- **Jackfruit:** With a fibrous and meaty texture, young or unripe jackfruit is used as a meat substitute in dishes like pulled pork or shredded chicken.
- **Eggplant (Aubergine):** When cooked, eggplant takes on a meaty texture and can be used in dishes like eggplant lasagna or grilled eggplant steaks.
- **Textured Vegetable Protein (TVP):** Made from soy flour, TVP comes in granules or chunks and can be rehydrated to resemble ground meat. It's often used in vegetarian and vegan dishes.

- **Quinoa:** This grain is high in protein and can be used as a base for various dishes, including salads, bowls, and stuffed vegetables.

- **Nuts and Seeds:** Almonds, walnuts, sunflower seeds, and pumpkin seeds can be ground or chopped to add a meaty texture to dishes.

- **Lentils:** Both brown and green lentils are popular choices for mimicking the texture of ground meat in dishes like tacos, chili, and spaghetti sauce.

- **Chickpea Flour (Besan):** Chickpea flour can be used to make a variety of dishes, including chickpea omelets and savory pancakes.

- **Vegetable Patties:** Commercially available veggie burgers and patties often contain a mix of vegetables, grains, and legumes to create a satisfying meat substitute.

- **Soy Products:** Apart from tofu and tempeh, soy-based products like soy crumbles and soy-based sausages are available as meat alternatives.

- **Beyond Meat and Impossible Burger:** These are plant-based burgers designed to closely resemble the taste and texture of traditional beef burgers.

These options cater to various dietary preferences, including vegetarian, vegan, and flexitarian diets. Keep in mind that the availability of these substitutes may vary depending on your location and the products offered by local retailers.

Here are ten recipes for vegetable patties that you can try. Put all the ingredients into a mixing bowl with a dough hook or mix by hand. The dough hook helps along the binding process to hold the patties together.

VIBRANT VEGGIE DELIGHTS: A VEGETARIAN CULINARY JOURNEY

Quinoa and Black Bean Patties

- 1 cup cooked Quinoa
- 1 cup cooked Black Beans
- ½ cup Bell Pepper chopped
- ½ cup Vidalia Onion chopped finely
- 3 cloves chopped fresh Garlic
- ½ cup Seasoned Breadcrumbs
- ¼ cup Fresh Chopped Parsley
- 1 egg (optional as a binder) adding a bit of water helps if needed.
- Salt and pepper to taste.

Throw it all together and mix till a consistency is reached to form patties. Cooking the patties will release the aromatics from the vegetables and tighten it up especially if you use the egg.

Sweet Potato and Chickpea Patties

- 1 cup Sweet Potatoes cooked and cooled
- 1 cup Chickpeas cooked and drained. Canned works
- ½ cup diced Red Bell Peppers
- ½ cup diced Red Onion
- 1 Tbsp diced garlic
- ½ cup Breadcrumbs
- 1 tbsp chili powder
- Salt and Pepper to taste

Broccoli and Cheddar Patties

- 1 cup cooked and chopped Broccoli
- 1 cup shredded Cheddar Cheese
- ½ cup chopped green onion
- ½ cup chopped fresh Basil
- ½ cup Breadcrumbs
- 1 beaten egg
- Salt and Pepper to taste

Zucchini and Feta Patties

- 1 cup raw shredded Zucchini
- 1 cup of Feta Cheese
- ½ cup breadcrumbs
- 2 Tbsp fresh Dill
- 2 Tbs Fresh Mint
- 1 egg
- Salt and pepper to taste

As you can see the recipes are similar and I encourage you to experiment with other fun combinations. If you are Vegan, substitute the egg for some flour and a bit of water (enough to get the consistency you are looking for in your patties) obviously it will vary with the amount of moisture in your veggies. Here are a few more combinations for you to play with.

VIBRANT VEGGIE DELIGHTS: A VEGETARIAN CULINARY JOURNEY

Eggplant and Chickpea Patties

- **Ingredients:** Eggplant, chickpeas, red onion, garlic, cumin, coriander, flour, egg, salt, and pepper.

Mushroom and Walnut Patties

- **Ingredients:** Mushrooms, walnuts, onion, garlic, breadcrumbs, thyme, egg, salt, and pepper.

Kale and White Bean Patties

- **Ingredients:** Kale, white beans, onion, garlic, breadcrumbs, lemon zest, egg, salt, and pepper.

Feel free to customize!

IMPOSSIBLE BURGERS

The Impossible Burger is a plant-based burger designed to replicate the taste and texture of traditional meat burgers. The recipe differ since then, but as of my last update, the common ingredients in the Impossible Burger include:

- **Water:** A primary component to form the base of the burger.
- **Soy Protein Concentrate:** Derived from soybeans, this ingredient provides a protein source that contributes to the burger's texture.
- **Coconut Oil:** Adds richness and helps replicate the juicy quality of traditional beef burgers.
- **Sunflower Oil:** Another source of healthy fats, contributing to the burger's moistness.
- **Natural Flavors:** These are proprietary blends of flavors that aim to mimic the taste of beef.
- **2% or Less of:** This category includes various other ingredients, such as:
- **Potato Protein:** Contributes to the burger's texture.
- **Methylcellulose:** Acts as a binder, helping to hold the ingredients together.
- **Yeast Extract:** Adds savory, umami flavors.
- **Cultured Dextrose:** A type of sugar used to enhance flavor.

- **Food Starch Modified:** This can be derived from various sources and is used as a thickening agent.
- **Soy Leghemoglobin (heme):** This is a key ingredient that gives the Impossible Burger a meat-like flavor and helps it "bleed" like real meat.

The Impossible Burger is a plant-based burger that aims to mimic the taste and texture of traditional beef burgers. Keep in mind that the exact recipe for the Impossible Burger is proprietary, but you can create a similar plant-based burger at home. Here's a basic recipe for a homemade plant-based burger patty:

Ingredients:

- 1 1/2 cups cooked black beans, drained and rinsed
- 1 cup finely chopped mushrooms (such as cremini or shiitake)
- 1/2 cup finely chopped onion
- 2 cloves garlic, minced
- 1 Tablespoon soy sauce
- 1 Tablespoon tomato paste
- 1 Teaspoon smoked paprika
- 1 Teaspoon dried oregano
- 1/2 Teaspoon cumin
- 1/4 Teaspoon black pepper
- 1 cup cooked quinoa or cooked brown rice
- 1/2 cup breadcrumbs
- 1 flax egg (1 Tablespoon ground flax seed mixed with 3 Tablespoons water, let sit for 5 minutes)

Instructions:

In a large mixing bowl, mash the black beans with a fork or potato masher until mostly smooth, leaving some chunks for texture.

In a skillet over medium heat, sauté the chopped mushrooms, onions, and garlic until softened and any liquid from the mushrooms has evaporated.

Add the cooked mushroom mixture to the mashed black beans. Stir in soy sauce, tomato paste, smoked paprika, dried oregano, cumin, black pepper, and liquid smoke (if using).

Mix in the cooked quinoa or brown rice, breadcrumbs, and fax egg. Combine well until the mixture holds together.

Divide the mixture into equal portions and shape them into burger patties.

Heat a non-stick skillet or grill pan over medium-high heat. Cook the patties for about 4-5 minutes per side or until they develop a golden crust.

Serve the plant-based patties on your favorite burger buns with your choice of toppings, such as lettuce, tomatoes, pickles, and vegan mayonnaise.

VIBRANT VEGGIE DELIGHTS: A VEGETARIAN CULINARY JOURNEY

Classic Impossible Burger

- Plant-based ground beef substitute (like Beyond Meat or Impossible Burger)
- Salt and pepper to taste

Black Bean and Quinoa Impossible Burger

- 1 cup Black beans (canned or cooked)
- 1 cup Cooked quinoa
- ½ cup Diced Onion,
- Spices (cumin, chili powder} to taste
- Salt and pepper to taste

Mix all ingredients together (preferably with a mixing bowl with a dough hook) until the Beans and Quinoa are bound together to form patties.

Mushroom and Lentil Impossible Burger

- 1 cup Lentils (cooked and drained)
- 1 cup Mushrooms (finely chopped) uncooked
- ½ cup Green Onion
- ½ cup Bread crumbs
- Spices (thyme, rosemary garlic powder) to taste

VIBRANT VEGGIE DELIGHTS: A VEGETARIAN CULINARY JOURNEY

Chickpea and Spinach Impossible Burger

- Chickpeas (canned or cooked)
- Chopped spinach (cooked and drained)
- Onion, garlic
- Flour (to bind)
- Spices (coriander, cumin)
- Toppings of choice (vegan tzatziki, cucumber, red onion)

Sweet Potato and Black Bean Impossible Burger

- Sweet potatoes (cooked and mashed)
- Black beans (canned or cooked)
- Onion, garlic
- Spices (cumin, smoked paprika)
- Toppings of choice (vegan chipotle mayo, avocado)

Thai Inspired Impossible Burger

- Textured vegetable protein (TVP)
- Thai curry paste
- Soy sauce
- Lime juice
- Toppings of choice (pickled vegetables, cilantro)

VIBRANT VEGGIE DELIGHTS: A VEGETARIAN CULINARY JOURNEY

BBQ Jackfruit Impossible Burger

- Jackfruit (canned or fresh)
- BBQ sauce
- Onion, garlic
- Coleslaw (for topping)

Seitan and Mushroom

- Impossible Burger: Seitan (store-bought or homemade wheat gluten) Mushrooms (finely chopped)

Beet and Walnut Impossible Burger

- Beets (cooked and grated)
- Walnuts (finely chopped)
- Onion, garlic
- Spices (fennel, thyme)

Sushi Inspired Impossible Burger

- Edamame (blended)
- Nori (seaweed) fakes
- Soy sauce
- Ginger, garlic

Remember, these recipes are just starting points, and you can customize them based on your taste preferences. Additionally, various commercial plant-based meat products are available that can be used as a base for these Burgers.

JACKFRUIT IMPOSSIBLE BURGER.

Making a Jackfruit Impossible Burger is a creative and tasty alternative to traditional meat-based burgers. The combination of jackfruit and other plant-based ingredients can mimic the texture and flavor of meat. Here's a recipe for you:

Ingredients:

For the Jackfruit Patty

- 2 cans of young green jackfruit in brine or water, drained and rinsed
- 1 Tablespoon vegetable oil
- 1 small onion, finely chopped
- 2 cloves garlic, minced
- 1 Teaspoon smoked paprika
- 1 Teaspoon cumin powder
- 1/2 Teaspoon chili powder (adjust to taste)
- Salt and pepper to taste
- 1/4 cup barbecue sauce
- 1/4 cup tomato paste or ketchup
- 1 Tablespoon soy sauce or tamari
- 1 Tablespoon Worcestershire sauce (make sure it's vegan)
- 1 Tablespoon maple syrup or agave nectar

To Serve:

- Burger buns
- Lettuce, tomato, onion, pickles, or any other desired toppings

Instructions:

Prepare Jackfruit:

- Shred the jackfruit using your hands or a fork, removing any seeds.
- Heat oil in a pan over medium heat. Add chopped onion and garlic, sauté until softened.
- Add shredded jackfruit to the pan and cook for about 5 minutes, stirring occasionally.
- Add smoked paprika, cumin powder, chili powder, salt, and pepper. Stir to combine.

Sauce Mixture:

- In a small bowl, mix barbecue sauce, tomato paste (or ketchup), soy sauce, Worcestershire sauce, and maple syrup.

Combine and Simmer:

- Pour the sauce mixture over the jackfruit. Stir well to coat evenly.
- Reduce heat to low, cover, and let it simmer for 15-20 minutes, stirring occasionally. This allows the jackfruit to absorb the flavors.

Mash and Form Patties:

- Using a potato masher or fork, mash the jackfruit to create a texture resembling pulled meat.
- Form the mixture into patties and place them on a parchment-lined tray.

Cook Patties:

- You can either bake the patties in the oven or cook them on a stovetop. For baking, preheat the oven to 375°F (190°C) and bake for 20-25 minutes, flipping halfway. For the stovetop, cook each side on a lightly oiled pan until golden brown.

Assemble Burgers:

- Serve your Jackfruit Impossible Burgers hot and enjoy!

Feel free to customize the recipe to your liking, and don't forget to add your favorite sauces, condiments, and toppings. Enjoy!

TEMPEH

Tempeh is a traditional Indonesian soy product that is made by fermenting soybeans. The fermentation process involves the use of a specific mold called Rhizopus oligosporus, which binds the soybeans into a compact cake-like form. Here's a basic overview of how tempeh is made:

Tempeh Making Process:

Ingredients:

- Soybeans
- Tempeh starter culture (Rhizopus oligosporus)
- Vinegar or another acid

Preparing Soybeans:

- Soybeans are soaked in water for several hours, usually overnight, to soften them.

Cooking Soybeans:

- The soaked soybeans are then boiled or steamed until they are fully cooked
- The cooked soybeans are cooled, and a tempeh starter culture containing the Rhizopus oligosporus mold is mixed in. Vinegar or another acid is often added to create an acidic environment that flavors the growth of the mold.

Incubation:

- The inoculated soybeans are then packed into a container and left to ferment in a warm environment (usually around 86°F or 30°C) for about 24 to 48 hours. During this time, the mold grows and binds the soybeans together into a firm, dense cake.

Harvesting:

Once the tempeh is fully fermented, it is ready to be harvested and can be sliced or used in various recipes.

Five Common Tempeh Recipes:

Grilled Tempeh Skewers

- Marinate tempeh cubes in a mixture of soy sauce, garlic, ginger, and a touch of maple syrup. Skewer them and grill until golden brown.

Tempeh Stir Fry

- Cube tempeh and stir-fry with your favorite vegetables, such as bell peppers, broccoli, and snap peas.
- Add a savory sauce made from soy sauce, sesame oil, and ginger.

Tempeh Tacos

- Crumble tempeh and cook it with taco seasoning. Serve in taco shells with your favorite toppings like lettuce, tomatoes, salsa, and guacamole.

Tempeh Curry

- Cut tempeh into cubes and simmer in a flavorful curry sauce made with coconut milk, curry spices, and vegetables.

Tempeh Salad Bowl

- Slice tempeh and pan-fry until crispy. Place it on top of a salad bowl with mixed greens, cherry tomatoes, avocado, and your choice of dressing.

Feel free to adjust these recipes based on your preferences and dietary restrictions. Tempeh is versatile and can be used in a variety of dishes.

It's important to note that the exact formula and ingredients may have changed, as companies often refine their recipes. Always check the product packaging or the manufacturer's website for the most up-to-date information.

Soy is a versatile legume that is commonly used to create a variety of plant-based products, making it a popular choice for vegetarians. Here are some main soy products available to vegetarians:

MAJOR SOY PRODUCTS AVAILABLE

- **Tofu (Bean Curd):** Tofu is a soybean-based product made by coagulating soy milk and pressing the curds into soft, firm, or extra firm blocks. It has a mild flavor and a texture that can range from silky to firm, making it adaptable to various dishes.

- **Tempeh:** Tempeh is a fermented soybean product that originates from Indonesia. It has a nutty flavor and a firm, dense texture. Tempeh is often used as a meat substitute in various dishes and is rich in protein.

- **Edamame:** Edamame are young, green soybeans that are typically harvested before they fully mature. They are often served in their pods and are a popular snack or appetizer. Edamame is also available shelled and can be added to salads, stir-fries, or other dishes.

- **Soy Milk:** Soy milk is a plant-based milk alternative made from soybeans. It is a good source of protein, and many varieties are fortified with vitamins and minerals, such as calcium and vitamin D. Soy milk can be used as a substitute for cow's milk in a variety of recipes.

- **Soy Yogurt:** Similar to soy milk, soy yogurt is a dairy-free alternative made from soybeans. It is fermented with beneficial bacteria to create a creamy, yogurt-like consistency. Soy yogurt can be enjoyed on its own or used in smoothies, desserts, and other dishes.

- **Soy Sauce:** While not a protein source, soy sauce is a popular condiment made from fermented soybeans. It adds savory and umami flavors to a variety of dishes and is a staple in many Asian cuisines.

- **Soy Protein Isolate and Textured Vegetable Protein (TVP):** textured Vegetable Protein (TVP) is a high-protein meat substitute made from soy flour. It is also known as textured soy protein, soy meat, or soya chunks. TVP is popular among vegetarians and vegans as a versatile and cost-effective protein source. Here are some key points about Textured Vegetable Protein:

Source and Production:

- TVP is typically made from defatted soy flour, which is a by-product of soybean oil extraction.
- The soy flour is mixed with water and then extruded to form various shapes, such as granules, chunks, fakes, or strips.
- After extrusion, the product is often dehydrated to remove the moisture, resulting in a lightweight and shelf-stable protein product.

Versatility:

- One of the main advantages of TVP is its versatility. It has a neutral flavor on its own, allowing it to absorb the flavors of the dishes it is cooked with.
- TVP can be used as a meat substitute in a variety of dishes, including chili, stews, tacos, spaghetti sauce, burgers, and more.

Storage and Shelf Life:

- TVP has a long shelf life and is easy to store. It is often sold in dry form and can be kept in a cool, dry place.
- Rehydrated TVP can be refrigerated for a few days or frozen for longer-term storage.

Environmental Impact:

- Soy-based products, including TVP, are often considered more environmentally sustainable than animal-based protein sources due to the lower environmental impact associated with soy cultivation compared to livestock farming.

VIBRANT VEGGIE DELIGHTS: A VEGETARIAN CULINARY JOURNEY

Quinoa Stuffed Bell PeppersC

Ingreditents

- 4 large bell peppers (any color)
- 1 cup quinoa, rinsed
- 2 cups vegetable broth or water
- 1 tablespoon olive oil
- 1 small onion, finely chopped
- 2 cloves garlic, minced
- 1 medium zucchini, diced
- 1 medium tomato, diced
- 1/2 cup corn kernels (fresh, canned, or frozen)
- 1/2 cup black beans, drained and rinsed
- 1 teaspoon ground cumin
- 1 teaspoon chili powder
- Salt and pepper to taste
- 1 cup shredded cheese (cheddar, mozzarella, or your choice)
- Fresh cilantro or parsley for garnish (optional)

Instructions

- Preheat your oven to 375°F (190°C). Line a baking dish with parchment paper or lightly grease it with olive oil.
- Cut the tops off the bell peppers and remove the seeds and membranes. Place the peppers in the prepared baking dish, cut side up.

- In a medium saucepan, combine the quinoa and vegetable broth or water. Bring to a boil, then reduce the heat to low, cover, and simmer for about 15 minutes, or until the quinoa is cooked and the liquid is absorbed. Remove from heat and set aside.

- In a large skillet, heat the olive oil over medium heat. Add the onion and garlic and sauté until softened, about 3-4 minutes.

- Add the diced zucchini, tomato, corn, and black beans to the skillet. Stir in the ground cumin, chili powder, salt, and pepper. Cook for another 5 minutes, or until the vegetables are tender.

- Add the cooked quinoa to the skillet and stir to combine everything well. Adjust seasoning if necessary.

- Spoon the quinoa mixture into the prepared bell peppers, packing it down gently with the back of the spoon. Top each stuffed pepper with shredded cheese.

- Cover the baking dish with foil and bake in the preheated oven for 25-30 minutes, or until the peppers are tender and the cheese is melted and bubbly.

- Remove from the oven and let cool for a few minutes before serving. Garnish with fresh cilantro or parsley

VIBRANT VEGGIE DELIGHTS: A VEGETARIAN CULINARY JOURNEY

Sweet Potato and Chickpea Curry

Ingredients

- 2 medium sweet potatoes, peeled and diced
- 1 can (15 oz) chickpeas, drained and rinsed
- 1 onion, diced
- 2 cloves garlic, minced
- 1 tablespoon fresh ginger, minced
- 1 can (14 oz) coconut milk
- 1 can (14 oz) diced tomatoes
- 1 tablespoon curry powder
- 1 teaspoon ground cumin
- 1 teaspoon ground coriander
- 1/2 teaspoon turmeric
- 1/4 teaspoon cayenne pepper (adjust to taste)
- Salt and pepper to taste
- 2 tablespoons oil (olive oil or coconut oil)
- Fresh cilantro for garnish (optional)
- Cooked rice or naan bread for serving

Instructions

- Heat the oil in a large skillet or pot over medium heat. Add the diced onion and cook until softened, about 5 minutes.
- Add the minced garlic and ginger to the skillet and cook for another minute until fragrant.
- Stir in the curry powder, cumin, coriander, turmeric, and cayenne pepper. Cook for about 1 minute, stirring constantly, until the spices are fragrant.
- Add the diced sweet potatoes to the skillet and stir to coat them with the spice mixture.
- Pour in the coconut milk and diced tomatoes with their juices. Stir to combine everything.
- Bring the mixture to a simmer, then reduce the heat to low and cover the skillet. Let the curry cook for about 15-20 minutes, or until the sweet potatoes are tender.
- Once the sweet potatoes are tender, add the drained and rinsed chickpeas to the skillet. Stir to combine and let the curry simmer for another 5 minutes to heat the chickpeas through.
- Season the curry with salt and pepper to taste.
- Serve the sweet potato and chickpea curry hot over cooked rice or with naan bread. Garnish with fresh cilantro if desired.

Mushroom and Spinach Stuffed Shells

Sure! Here's a delicious recipe for mushroom and spinach stuffed shells:

Ingredients:

- 1 box of jumbo pasta shells
- 2 cups of chopped mushrooms (any variety you prefer)
- 2 cups of fresh spinach, chopped
- 2 cloves of garlic, minced
- 1 small onion, finely chopped
- 1 cup of ricotta cheese
- 1 cup of shredded mozzarella cheese
- 1/2 cup of grated Parmesan cheese
- 1 egg, lightly beaten
- 2 tablespoons of olive oil
- Salt and pepper to taste
- 1 jar (about 24 oz) of your favorite marinara sauce

Instructions:

- Preheat your oven to 350°F (175°C).
- Cook the jumbo pasta shells according to the package instructions. Make sure to cook them al dente. Drain and set aside to cool.
- In a large skillet, heat the olive oil over medium heat. Add the chopped onions and minced garlic, sautéing until fragrant and translucent, about 2-3 minutes.

- Add the chopped mushrooms to the skillet and cook until they release their moisture and become tender, about 5-7 minutes.

- Stir in the chopped spinach and cook until wilted, about 2-3 minutes. Season with salt and pepper to taste. Remove from heat and let the mixture cool slightly.

- In a large mixing bowl, combine the ricotta cheese, shredded mozzarella cheese, grated Parmesan cheese, and beaten egg. Mix until well combined.

- Fold the mushroom and spinach mixture into the cheese mixture until evenly distributed.

- Spread a thin layer of marinara sauce on the bottom of a 9x13 inch baking dish.

- Stuff each cooked pasta shell with a generous spoonful of the mushroom and spinach mixture and place them in the baking dish, arranging them in a single layer.

- Once all the shells are stuffed and placed in the baking dish, pour the remaining marinara sauce over the top, covering the shells evenly.

- Cover the baking dish with aluminum foil and bake in the preheated oven for 25-30 minutes, or until the shells are heated through and the sauce is bubbling.

- Remove the foil and sprinkle some extra shredded mozzarella cheese on top. Return to the oven and bake for an additional 5-7 minutes, or until the cheese is melted and lightly golden.

- Once done, remove from the oven and let it cool for a few minutes before serving. Garnish with fresh parsley or basil if desired.

VIBRANT VEGGIE DELIGHTS: A VEGETARIAN CULINARY JOURNEY

Vegetarian Sushi Bowls

Ingredients:

- 2 cups sushi rice
- 4 cups water
- 1/2 cup rice vinegar
- 2 tablespoons sugar
- 1 teaspoon salt
- 1 avocado, sliced
- 1 cucumber, julienned
- 1 carrot, julienned
- 1/2 cup edamame, cooked and shelled
- 1/4 cup pickled ginger
- 1/4 cup soy sauce
- 2 tablespoons sesame seeds (black or white), toasted
- Optional toppings: sliced radishes, sliced green onions, seaweed salad

Instructions:

- Rinse the sushi rice under cold water until the water runs clear. In a medium saucepan, combine the rice and water. Bring to a boil over high heat, then reduce the heat to low, cover, and simmer for 18-20 minutes, or until the rice is tender and the water is absorbed.

- In a small saucepan, combine the rice vinegar, sugar, and salt. Heat over medium heat until the sugar and salt are dissolved. Remove from heat.

- Transfer the cooked rice to a large bowl and pour the vinegar mixture over it. Gently fold the vinegar mixture into the rice until well combined. Let the rice cool to room temperature.

- Assemble the sushi bowls: Divide the sushi rice among four bowls. Top each bowl with avocado slices, cucumber, carrot, edamame, and pickled ginger.

- Drizzle each bowl with soy sauce and sprinkle with toasted sesame seeds.

- Add any optional toppings you like, such as sliced radishes, green onions, or seaweed salad.

- Serve immediately and enjoy your vegetarian sushi bowls!

- Feel free to adjust the toppings to your taste preferences, and you can also add other ingredients like tofu, tempura vegetables, or marinated mushrooms for extra flavor and texture.

Eggplant Parmesan Roll Ups

Ingredients:

- 1 large eggplant
- 1 cup marinara sauce
- 1 cup ricotta cheese
- 1 cup shredded mozzarella cheese
- 1/2 cup grated Parmesan cheese
- 2 cloves garlic, minced
- 2 tablespoons chopped fresh basil
- 1 tablespoon chopped fresh parsley

- Salt and pepper to taste
- Olive oil for frying
- Toothpicks

Instructions:

- Preheat Oven: Preheat your oven to 375°F (190°C).
- Prepare the Eggplant: Slice the eggplant lengthwise into thin strips, about 1/4 inch thick with a mandolin. You should get about 8-10 slices depending on the size of the eggplant. Sprinkle both sides of each slice with salt and let them sit for about 15-20 minutes to draw out excess moisture. Afterward, pat them dry with paper towels.
- Heat some olive oil in a large skillet over medium heat. Fry the eggplant slices in batches until they are tender and lightly browned on both sides, about 2-3 minutes per side. Transfer them to a plate lined with paper towels to drain any excess oil.
- In a mixing bowl, combine the ricotta cheese, minced garlic, chopped basil, chopped parsley, half of the shredded mozzarella cheese, and half of the grated Parmesan cheese. Mix well.
- Spread a spoonful of marinara sauce onto each eggplant slice. Then, spread a generous spoonful of the ricotta mixture on top of the sauce. Carefully roll up each slice and secure it with a toothpick.
- Place the eggplant roll-ups seam side down in a baking dish. Pour the remaining marinara sauce over the top of the roll-ups and sprinkle the remaining mozzarella and Parmesan cheese on top. Cover the baking dish with aluminum foil and bake in the preheated oven for about 20-25 minutes, until the cheese is melted and bubbly.

VIBRANT VEGGIE DELIGHTS: A VEGETARIAN CULINARY JOURNEY

Chickpea and Vegetable Stir Fry

Ingredients:

- 1 can (15 ounces) chickpeas, drained and rinsed
- 2 cups mixed vegetables (such as bell peppers, broccoli, carrots, snap peas)
- 2 cloves garlic, minced
- 1 small onion, thinly sliced
- 2 tablespoons soy sauce (or tamari for gluten-free option)
- 1 tablespoon sesame oil
- 1 tablespoon olive oil
- 1 teaspoon grated ginger
- 1/2 teaspoon red pepper flakes (optional)
- Cooked rice or noodles, for serving
- Salt and pepper to taste
- Chopped green onions and sesame seeds for garnish (optional)

Instructions

- Rinse and drain the chickpeas. Chop all the vegetables into bite-sized pieces. Mince the garlic and ginger.
- Heat olive oil in a large skillet or wok over medium-high heat. Add minced garlic and ginger, and stir-fry for about 30 seconds until fragrant.
- Add the mixed vegetables to the skillet. Stir-fry for about 3-4 minutes until they are tender-crisp.
- Add the chickpeas to the skillet with the vegetables. Stir well to combine.
- Pour soy sauce and sesame oil over the mixture. Stir everything together until the chickpeas and vegetables are coated evenly. Season with salt and pepper to taste.
- Continue cooking for another 2-3 minutes until everything is heated through and the flavors have melded together.
- Serve the chickpea and vegetable stir-fry hot over cooked rice or noodles if desired. Garnish with sesame seeds, chopped green onions, or cilantro for added flavor and presentation.
- Who doesn't like a good curry dish? For the sake of not leaving anyone out here are a couple that are pretty easy and very tasty.

VIBRANT VEGGIE DELIGHTS: A VEGETARIAN CULINARY JOURNEY

Lentil and Vegetable Coconut Curry

Ingredients:

- 1 cup dried lentils (any variety you prefer)
- 1 tablespoon coconut oil
- 1 onion, diced
- 3 cloves garlic, minced
- 1 tablespoon grated ginger
- 2 carrots, diced
- 1 bell pepper, diced
- 1 zucchini, diced
- 1 can (14 oz) coconut milk
- 1 can (14 oz) diced tomatoes
- 2 tablespoons curry powder
- 1 teaspoon ground turmeric
- 1 teaspoon ground cumin
- Salt and pepper to taste
- Fresh cilantro for garnish (optional)
- Cooked rice or naan bread for serving

Instructions:

- Rinse the lentils under cold water and drain them.
- In a large pot, heat the coconut oil over medium heat. Add the diced onion and cook until softened, about 5 minutes.
- Add the minced garlic and grated ginger to the pot, stirring constantly for about 1 minute until fragrant.
- Stir in the diced carrots, bell pepper, and zucchini. Cook for another 5 minutes, until the vegetables start to soften.
- Add the rinsed lentils to the pot along with the coconut milk and diced tomatoes. Stir well to combine.
- Add the curry powder, ground turmeric, and ground cumin to the pot, stirring to evenly distribute the spices.
- Season with salt and pepper to taste.
- Bring the curry to a simmer, then reduce the heat to low and let it cook, covered, for about 20-25 minutes, or until the lentils and vegetables are tender, stirring occasionally.
- Once cooked, taste and adjust seasoning if necessary.
- Serve the lentil and vegetable coconut curry hot, garnished with fresh cilantro if desired, alongside cooked rice or naan bread.
- Cook lentils with a variety of vegetables in a coconut milk-based curry sauce.
- Add curry spices, turmeric, and ginger for a flavorful and comforting dish.

Cauliflower Steaks

Ingredients

- 1 large cauliflower head
- 2-3 tablespoons olive oil
- 2 teaspoons garlic powder
- 1 teaspoon smoked paprika
- Salt and pepper to taste
- Optional: Lemon wedges for serving

Instructions

- Preheat your oven to 425°F (220°C).
- Remove the leaves from the cauliflower and trim the stem, leaving the core intact. Place the cauliflower head on a cutting board, core side down.
- Slice the cauliflower into 1-inch thick steaks. You should get 2-3 steaks from one head, depending on its size.
- In a small bowl, mix together olive oil, garlic powder, smoked paprika, salt, and pepper.
- Brush both sides of each cauliflower steak with the oil and spice mixture, ensuring they are well coated.
- Place the cauliflower steaks on a baking sheet lined with parchment paper or a silicone baking mat.
- Roast in the preheated oven for 25-30 minutes or until the cauliflower is golden brown and tender, flipping halfway through the cooking time.
- Remove from the oven and serve the cauliflower steaks hot. Squeeze a bit of lemon juice over them if desired.

Creamy Tomato Basil Soup

Ingredients

- 2 cans (28 oz each) crushed tomatoes
- 1 onion, finely chopped
- 3 cloves garlic, minced
- 4 cups vegetable broth
- 1 cup heavy cream or coconut milk for a dairy-free option
- 1/4 cup fresh basil, chopped
- Salt and pepper to taste

Instructions

- In a large pot, sauté the onions and garlic until translucent.
- Add crushed tomatoes and vegetable broth. Bring to a simmer.
- Stir in heavy cream or coconut milk and let it simmer for another 10 minutes.
- Add fresh basil, salt, and pepper. Blend the soup until smooth.
- Serve hot, garnished with additional basil if desired.

VIBRANT VEGGIE DELIGHTS: A VEGETARIAN CULINARY JOURNEY

Spicy Lentil Soup

Ingredients

- 1 cup dried red lentils, rinsed
- 1 onion, diced
- 2 carrots, chopped
- 3 cloves garlic, minced
- 1 can (14 oz) diced tomatoes
- 6 cups vegetable broth
- 1 teaspoon cumin
- 1/2 teaspoon paprika
- 1/4 teaspoon cayenne pepper
- Salt and pepper to taste

Instructions

- In a large pot, sauté onions and garlic until softened.
- Add carrots, lentils, diced tomatoes, and vegetable broth. Bring to a boil.
- Reduce heat and add cumin, paprika, cayenne pepper, salt, and pepper. Simmer until lentils are tender.
- Adjust seasoning if needed. Serve hot.

Coconut Curry Vegetable Soup

Ingredients

- 1 can (14 oz) coconut milk
- 4 cups vegetable broth
- 1 tablespoon red curry paste
- 1 cup broccoli florets
- 1 carrot, sliced
- 1 bell pepper, diced
- 1 cup mushrooms, sliced
- 1 cup spinach leaves
- 1 tablespoon soy sauce
- Rice noodles (optional)

Instructions

- In a pot, combine coconut milk, vegetable broth, and red curry paste. Bring to a simmer.
- Add broccoli, carrot, bell pepper, and mushrooms. Cook until vegetables are tender.
- Stir in spinach and soy sauce. If desired, add rice noodles and cook until noodles are done.
- Serve hot, garnished with cilantro.

Chickpea and Vegetable Soup

Ingredients

- 1 can (15 oz) chickpeas, drained and rinsed
- 1 onion, chopped
- 2 carrots, diced
- 2 celery stalks, sliced
- 3 cloves garlic, minced
- 6 cups vegetable broth
- 1 can (14 oz) diced tomatoes
- 1 teaspoon dried thyme
- 1 teaspoon dried rosemary
- Salt and pepper to taste

Instructions

- In a large pot, sauté onions and garlic until softened.
- Add carrots, celery, chickpeas, vegetable broth, diced tomatoes, thyme, rosemary, salt, and pepper.
- Simmer until vegetables are tender. Adjust seasoning if needed.
- Serve hot with crusty bread here are a few recipes for bread you can try.

Sweet potato and chickpea curry

Ingredients

- 2 tablespoons oil (coconut oil or vegetable oil)
- 1 onion, chopped
- 3 cloves garlic, minced
- 1 tablespoon fresh ginger, grated
- 2 medium sweet potatoes, peeled and diced
- 1 can (15 ounces) chickpeas, drained and rinsed
- 1 can (14 ounces) diced tomatoes
- 1 can (14 ounces) coconut milk
- 1 tablespoon curry powder
- 1 teaspoon ground cumin
- 1 teaspoon ground coriander
- 1/2 teaspoon turmeric powder
- 1/4 teaspoon cayenne pepper (optional, for extra heat)
- Salt and pepper to taste
- Fresh cilantro, chopped (for garnish)
- Cooked rice or naan bread (for serving)

Instructions

- Heat the oil in a large pot or skillet over medium heat. Add the chopped onion and cook until softened, about 5 minutes.
- Add the minced garlic and grated ginger to the pot, and cook for another 1-2 minutes until fragrant.
- Stir in the diced sweet potatoes and cook for 5 minutes, stirring occasionally.
- Add the drained chickpeas, diced tomatoes (with their juices), and coconut milk to the pot. Stir well to combine.
- Sprinkle the curry powder, ground cumin, ground coriander, turmeric powder, and cayenne pepper (if using) over the mixture. Stir until the spices are evenly distributed.
- Season with salt and pepper to taste, then bring the mixture to a simmer. Reduce the heat to low, cover the pot, and let the curry simmer for about 20-25 minutes, or until the sweet potatoes are tender.
- Once the sweet potatoes are cooked through, taste the curry and adjust the seasoning if needed.
- Serve the sweet potato and chickpea curry hot, garnished with fresh chopped cilantro. Enjoy with cooked rice or naan bread.

VIBRANT VEGGIE DELIGHTS: A VEGETARIAN CULINARY JOURNEY

Lentil and coconut curry

Ingredients

- 1 cup dried lentils (any variety you prefer)
- 1 tablespoon coconut oil
- 1 onion, diced
- 3 cloves garlic, minced
- 1 tablespoon ginger, minced
- 1 red bell pepper, diced
- 1 carrot, diced
- 1 tablespoon curry powder
- 1 teaspoon ground cumin
- 1 teaspoon ground coriander
- 1/2 teaspoon turmeric
- 1 can (14 oz) coconut milk
- 1 cup vegetable broth
- Salt and pepper to taste
- Fresh cilantro for garnish (optional)
- Serve with Cooked rice or Naan bread

Instructions

- Rinse the lentils under cold water and drain them. Set aside.
- In a large pot or Dutch oven, heat the coconut oil over medium heat.
- Add the diced onion and cook until translucent, about 5 minutes.
- Stir in the minced garlic and ginger, and cook for another 2 minutes until fragrant.
- Add the diced bell pepper and carrot to the pot, and cook for 5 minutes until they begin to soften.
- Stir in the curry powder, ground cumin, ground coriander, and turmeric, and cook for another minute to toast the spices.
- Add the rinsed lentils to the pot, along with the coconut milk and vegetable broth. Stir well to combine.
- Bring the mixture to a simmer, then reduce the heat to low and cover the pot. Let it simmer gently for about 20-25 minutes, or until the lentils are tender.
- Season the curry with salt and pepper to taste.
- Serve the lentil and coconut curry hot, garnished with fresh cilantro if desired, alongside cooked rice or naan bread.

VIBRANT VEGGIE DELIGHTS: A VEGETARIAN CULINARY JOURNEY

Spinach and feta stuffed portobello mushrooms

Ingredients

- 4 large portobello mushrooms
- 2 cups fresh spinach, chopped
- 1 small onion, finely chopped
- 2 cloves garlic, minced
- 1 tablespoon olive oil
- 1/2 cup crumbled feta cheese
- Salt and pepper to taste
- 1/4 cup breadcrumbs (optional, for topping)

Instructions

- Preheat your oven to 375°F (190°C).
- Clean the portobello mushrooms with a damp cloth to remove any dirt. Remove the stems and gently scrape out the gills using a spoon to create space for the stuffing.
- Heat olive oil in a pan over medium heat. Add the chopped onion and minced garlic. Sauté until the onion becomes translucent, about 2-3 minutes.
- Add the chopped spinach to the pan and cook until it wilts, about 2-3 minutes more. Season with salt and pepper to taste.
- Remove the pan from heat and let the mixture cool for a few minutes.
- Once the spinach mixture has cooled slightly, stir in the crumbled feta cheese.

- Spoon the spinach and feta mixture into each portobello mushroom, dividing it evenly among them.
- Place the stuffed mushrooms on a baking sheet lined with parchment paper or aluminum foil.
- If desired, sprinkle bread crumbs over the stuffed mushrooms for a crispy topping.
- Bake in the preheated oven for 15-20 minutes, or until the mushrooms are tender and the filling is heated through.
- Once done, remove the stuffed mushrooms from the oven and let them cool for a few minutes before serving.
- Garnish with fresh herbs like parsley or a sprinkle of extra feta cheese if desired.

Caprese salad skewers

Ingredients

- Fresh mozzarella balls (bocconcini), about 20
- Cherry tomatoes, about 20
- Fresh basil leaves, about 20
- Balsamic glaze (or balsamic reduction)
- Extra virgin olive oil
- Salt and pepper, to taste
- Wooden skewers

Instructions

- Rinse the cherry tomatoes and fresh basil leaves. Drain the mozzarella balls if they were stored in liquid.

- Take a wooden skewer and start by threading on a cherry tomato, followed by a folded basil leaf, and then a mozzarella ball. Repeat this process until the skewer is filled, leaving a little space at the end for easy handling. Repeat until you've used all the ingredients.

- Once all the skewers are assembled, arrange them on a serving platter. Drizzle extra virgin olive oil over the skewers.

- Using a spoon or a squeeze bottle, drizzle the balsamic glaze over the skewers in a zigzag pattern.

- Caprese salad skewers are best served fresh. Arrange them nicely on a platter and serve immediately as an appetizer or a light snack.

Fried cauliflower buffalo bites

Ingredients

- 1 medium head of cauliflower, cut into florets
- 1 cup all-purpose flour (or rice flour for a gluten-free option)
- 1 cup milk (or almond milk for a dairy-free option)
- 1 teaspoon garlic powder
- 1 teaspoon paprika
- Salt and pepper to taste
- 1 cup buffalo sauce (store-bought or homemade)

- 2 tablespoons butter (or vegan butter)
- Oil for frying (vegetable oil works well)

Instructions

- Wash the cauliflower and cut it into bite-sized florets, removing any tough stems.
- In a mixing bowl, combine the flour, garlic powder, paprika, salt, and pepper.
- Gradually whisk in the milk until you have a smooth batter. Adjust the consistency by adding more flour or milk as needed. The batter should coat the cauliflower florets evenly.
- Heat oil in a deep fryer or large skillet over medium-high heat.
- Dip each cauliflower floret into the batter, making sure it's evenly coated.
- Allow any excess batter to drip off before transferring the coated florets to the hot oil.
- Fry the cauliflower in batches, making sure not to overcrowd the pan. Fry until golden brown and crispy, about 4-5 minutes per batch.
- Remove the fried cauliflower with a slotted spoon and place them on a paper towel-lined plate to drain any excess oil.
- the Buffalo Sauce
- In a small saucepan, melt the butter over low heat.
- Once the butter is melted, add the buffalo sauce and stir until well combined. You can adjust the ratio of butter to buffalo sauce according to your taste preference. Transfer the fried cauliflower to a large mixing bowl. Pour buffalo sauce over the cauliflower and toss until each piece is evenly coated. Serve the fried cauliflower buffalo bites hot, garnished with chopped fresh parsley or celery sticks on the side.

Ratatouille

A classic French Provençal stewed vegetable dish originating from Nice.

Ingredients

- 1 large eggplant, diced
- 2 medium zucchinis, diced
- 1 large onion, chopped
- 2-3 bell peppers (red, yellow, or green), diced
- 4-5 ripe tomatoes, diced
- 4 cloves garlic, minced
- 2 tablespoons olive oil
- 1 teaspoon dried thyme
- 1 teaspoon dried oregano
- Salt and pepper to taste
- Fresh basil leaves, chopped (for garnish)

Instructions

- Heat olive oil in a large skillet or Dutch oven over medium heat.
- Add chopped onions and minced garlic to the skillet. Sauté until onions are translucent and garlic is fragrant, about 3-4 minutes.
- Add diced eggplant to the skillet. Cook for about 5-7 minutes until the eggplant begins to soften.

- Stir in diced bell peppers and continue cooking for another 5 minutes.

- Add diced zucchinis to the skillet and cook for an additional 3-4 minutes.

- Stir in diced tomatoes, dried thyme, and dried oregano. Season with salt and pepper to taste.

- Reduce heat to low, cover the skillet, and let the ratatouille simmer for about 20-25 minutes, stirring occasionally, until all the vegetables are tender and flavors have melded together.

- Once done, taste and adjust seasoning if necessary. If the ratatouille seems too dry, you can add a splash of water or vegetable broth to achieve your desired consistency.

- Remove from heat and let it cool slightly before serving.

- Garnish with chopped fresh basil leaves before serving. Ratatouille can be served hot, warm, or at room temperature and pairs well with crusty bread or over cooked grains like rice or quinoa. Enjoy your homemade ratatouille!

Zucchini Parmesan

- 2 medium zucchinis, sliced into 1/4-inch rounds

- 1 cup breadcrumbs (you can use store-bought or make your own by processing stale bread)

- 1/2 cup grated Parmesan cheese

- 1/2 teaspoon garlic powder

- 1/2 teaspoon dried oregano

- 1/2 teaspoon dried basil
- Salt and pepper to taste
- 2 eggs, beaten
- Olive oil spray

Instructions

- Preheat your oven to 400°F (200°C). Line a baking sheet with parchment paper or lightly grease it with olive oil.
- In a shallow dish, mix together the breadcrumbs, grated Parmesan cheese, garlic powder, dried oregano, dried basil, salt, and pepper.
- Dip each zucchini slice into the beaten eggs, then coat it evenly with the breadcrumb mixture. Place the coated zucchini slices in a single layer on the prepared baking sheet.
- Lightly spray the tops of the zucchini slices with olive oil spray. This will help them become crispy in the oven.
- Bake the zucchini slices in the preheated oven for about 20-25 minutes, or until they are golden brown and crispy.
- Once done, remove the zucchini slices from the oven and serve them hot. You can garnish with extra grated Parmesan cheese and fresh chopped parsley if desired.
- One of my favorite cold soups is borscht and it happens to be vegetarian so I am throwing it in. Here is a good one.

Ukrainian Borscht

Ingredients

- 2 medium beets, peeled and grated
- 4 cups beef or vegetable broth
- 1 onion, finely chopped
- 2 carrots, peeled and grated
- 2 potatoes, peeled and diced
- 2 cloves garlic, minced
- 1/2 cabbage, shredded
- 2 tablespoons tomato paste
- 2 tablespoons vegetable oil
- 1 tablespoon vinegar
- 1 bay leaf
- Salt and pepper to taste
- Sour cream and fresh dill for garnish

Instructions

- Heat vegetable oil in a large pot over medium heat. Add chopped onions and sauté until translucent.
- Add grated carrots and minced garlic to the pot. Cook for another 2-3 minutes until the carrots start to soften. Stir in grated beets and tomato

paste. Cook for 5-7 minutes, stirring occasionally.

- Pour in beef or vegetable broth and add diced potatoes and shredded cabbage. Bring the soup to a boil, then reduce the heat to low and let it simmer for about 20-25 minutes, or until the vegetables are tender.
- Season the soup with salt, pepper, vinegar, and add a bay leaf for extra flavor. Adjust seasoning to taste.
- Once the soup is ready, remove the bay leaf and serve hot, garnished with a dollop of sour cream and chopped fresh dill.

Growing up on Cape Cod I was surrounded by Seafood so when my mom introduced me to Seitan i was genuinely impressed to the point of deciding to make and sell it wholesale myself. That's when I started Seitan Farms specifically for Seitan only, at the beginning. Then I brought on a few more healthy purveyors like Sandra's Salsas, Cielo Pasta and California Olive oil up in Salem Ma.

Breads

"Ah, bread. The unsung hero of the kitchen, the carb-loaded confidante, the doughy delight that always rises to the occasion... unless you forget the yeast! It goes with everything and making your own always makes it taste better. Here are a few to try yourself if you got the oven for it!

Sourdough bread

Ingredients

- 1 cup active sourdough starter
- 3 cups bread flour
- 1 ½ teaspoons salt
- 1 cup lukewarm water

Instructions

- Mix the sourdough starter, flour, and salt in a bowl.
- Add water gradually, kneading until you have a smooth, elastic dough.
- Cover and let it rise at room temperature for 8-12 hours.
- Shape the dough, place it in a greased pan, and let it rise for another 1-2 hours.
- Preheat the oven to 450°F (230°C) and bake for 25-30 minutes.

Rye Bread

Ingredients

- 2 cups rye flour
- 2 cups bread flour
- 1 ½ teaspoons salt
- 1 tablespoon caraway seeds
- 1 tablespoon molasses
- 1 cup lukewarm water
- 2 ¼ teaspoons active dry yeast

Instructions

- Dissolve yeast in water and let it sit for 5 minutes.
- Mix flours, salt, caraway seeds, and molasses in a bowl.
- Add yeast mixture and knead until smooth. Let it rise for 1-2 hours.
- Shape the dough, place it in a greased pan, and let it rise for another 1-2 hours.
- Bake at 375°F (190°C) for 30-35 minutes.

Pumpernickel Bread

Ingredients

- 2 cups whole rye flour
- 1 cup bread flour
- 1 ½ teaspoons salt
- 1 tablespoon molasses
- 1 ½ teaspoons instant coffee
- 1 ¼ cups lukewarm water
- 2 ¼ teaspoons active dry yeast

Instructions

- Dissolve yeast in water with coffee and molasses. Let it sit for 5 minutes.
- Mix flours and salt in a bowl. Add the yeast mixture and knead until smooth.
- Let it rise for 1-2 hours. Shape the dough and let it rise again for 1-2 hours.
- Bake at 375°F (190°C) for 40-45 minutes.

Gluten Free Bread

Ingredients

- 2 cups gluten-free all-purpose flour
- 1 teaspoon xanthan gum
- 1 ½ teaspoons baking powder
- ½ teaspoon salt
- 1 ½ cups warm milk
- 2 tablespoons honey
- 2 ¼ teaspoons active dry yeast

Instructions

- Dissolve yeast in warm milk with honey. Let it sit for 5 minutes.
- Mix flour, xanthan gum, baking powder, and salt. Add the yeast mixture and mix well.
- Pour into a greased pan and let it rise for 30-40 minutes.
- Bake at 375°F (190°C) for 30-35 minutes.

VIBRANT VEGGIE DELIGHTS: A VEGETARIAN CULINARY JOURNEY

Artisanal Bread

Ingredients

- 3 ½ cups bread flour
- 2 teaspoons salt
- 1 ½ cups lukewarm water
- 1 ½ teaspoons active dry yeast

Instructions

- Dissolve yeast in water and let it sit for 5 minutes.
- Mix flour and salt. Add the yeast mixture and knead until smooth.
- Let it rise for 1-2 hours. Shape the dough and let it rise again for 1-2 hours.
- Preheat the oven to 450°F (230°C) and bake for 25-30 minutes.

Summary

A meat-free diet, often referred to as a vegetarian or plant-based diet, can offer a variety of health, environmental, and ethical benefits. It's important to note that the extent of these benefits can vary based on individual dietary choices and overall lifestyle. Here are some potential benefits:

As we are all probably aware of the health benefits of Plant-based diets. They are associated with lower levels of cholesterol and blood pressure, reducing the risk of heart disease. Vegetarian diets are often linked to lower body mass index (BMI) and a reduced risk of obesity. A diet rich in plant-based foods tends to be lower in calories and saturated fats.

Research suggests that a plant-based diet may reduce the risk of certain chronic diseases, including type 2 diabetes, certain cancers, and hypertension.

Increased Nutrient Intake: A well-balanced vegetarian diet can provide ample nutrients such as fiber, vitamins (e.g., vitamin C, vitamin E), minerals (e.g., potassium, magnesium), and antioxidants.

Plant-based diets, especially those rich in fiber from fruits, vegetables, and whole grains, can also contribute to a healthier digestive system and reduce the risk of constipation. The production of plant-based foods generally has a lower environmental impact compared to the production of animal-based foods. Reduced meat consumption can help conserve water, reduce deforestation, and lower greenhouse gas emissions.

Many people adopt a meat-free diet for ethical reasons, including concerns about animal welfare and the treatment of animals in the meat industry.

Support for Biodiversity: Plant-based diets often require less land for cultivation, reducing the pressure on ecosystems. This can contribute to the conservation of biodiversity. The use of antibiotics in animal agriculture can contribute to antibiotic resistance. Choosing a plant-based diet can help reduce the demand for antibiotic use in livestock.

Plant-based diets may be more cost-effective for individuals and families as plant-based foods often cost less than meat and dairy products.

It's important to note that while a well-planned vegetarian or vegan diet can be nutritionally adequate, individuals should pay attention to their nutrient intake, particularly regarding vitamin B12, iron, calcium, omega-3 fatty acids, and protein. Consulting with a healthcare professional or registered dietitian can help ensure a balanced and healthy meat-free diet.

So there you have it dear reader. A whole lot of information on meat substitutes. stay tuned for more books forthcoming beginning with Pestos! I have had my ear to the ground with regard to food for decades and am happy to share. So long for now.

ABOUT THE AUTHOR

Mike Feeney is a chef of 20 years in restaurants on Cape Cod, in Massachusetts as well as Florida including The Ocean Reef Club in Key Largo, Florida. Host of Feeneys Fantastic Finds At 5e61.com there is a collection of cool finds from wine club, to performance blogging and the latest fashion even high protein popcorn for workout snacks. Health and beauty products are also available as well as Biohacking supplements so definitely visit.